Spark
Provoking Radical
People-Centered
Innovation

Corey Pruitt

Spark
Provoking Radical People-Centered Innovation

By Corey Pruitt

A Publication of ChangeSparx, LLC - Phoenix, Arizona

http://www.ChangeSparx.com

Unattributed quotations are by Corey Pruitt

Edited by: Terri Plucker

Cover design by: Corey Pruitt

Printed in the United States of America

ISBN: 172085937X
ISBN-13: 978-1720859376

Contents

Chapter 1

Let's Get Started

Today's business market is different than ever before. Companies, in all fields, are opening their doors and closing their doors at record rates. Speed to market, from idea conception to launch, has been remarkably abbreviated. The complexion of today's consumer is incessantly evolving and morphing. Leaders in every industry, field, and market are endlessly being asked to produce more, produce quicker, and to innovate, innovate, innovate.

We can all come up with numerous examples of industry leaders who failed to innovate and have been left behind. I can still recall the sensory overload of rows and rows of movie covers adorning the yellow and blue walls at a certain Blockbuster video store. Heck, Blockbuster was a weekend night tradition for most families! Enter Netflix who changed up the video renting game and decided to send videos to the consumer (via mail and streaming) instead of having the consumer trek to the video store. Blockbuster saw their demise coming (and even had a chance to purchase Netflix) but decided to stay their course…all the way to bankruptcy.

Borders Books failed to change their focus and did not adopt new reading technologies like their competitors (Amazon and Barnes and Noble) did. Borders, seemingly, completely missed that reading would become an electronic experience from a tablet, phone or web browser for many consumers.

The popular toy store mammoth, Toys-R-Us, filed bankruptcy and started closing up shop in early 2018. There are, of course, many reasons for this and they relate directly to lack of innovation and iteration in their business model, in how they serve their consumer base and not fully adapting to the consumers' ever-evolving buying behaviors. Look at entire industries being disrupted by technology and innovation. Industries such as, the publishing industry (example: Amazon's CreateSpace), music industry (example: Apple iPod), transportation industry (example: Uber and Lyft), higher education (example: Southern New Hampshire University and Rio Salado College), photography (example: Apple iPhone), media/entertainment (example: Netflix, Hulu, and Amazon), personal hygiene products (example: Axe), and retail (Amazon, Wayfair, Overstock), just to name a few, have felt the effects of innovation.

Speculation Station

We could spend pages speculating as to why these companies (or industries) did not innovate as quickly (or at all) as their competitors, but that has been done already. There are many great books that share the numerous reasons why companies at the top often don't stay there. I have taken the liberty of generating a short list of potential reasons, but won't spend much time in this space of reasons why companies or industries did not innovate:

- Fixating on current successful offerings without accepting something better can (and will) come along.

- Focusing on the consumer/market of today without anticipating the future needs, wants and expectations of the consumer/market of the future.

- Failure to renovate technology, systems or equipment and change with the times which prevents the pursuit of newer, more relevant investments.

These, of course, are just a few of the major influencers in the "lack of innovation" space. And, these certainly need to be avoided!

So, how do we avoid the common organizational deterioration that so many leaders and companies have to deal with?

Well that is the focus of this book. Throughout these pages you will journey through the five sparks of a people-centered innovation atmosphere, and how to implement them into your organization. You will journey through the 8 Brain Blocks that may be sabotaging your ability to generate, develop and implement new and creative ideas. Throughout these pages you will journey through the process of harnessing the immense power of your brain to spark innovation through one very powerful tool.

The innovation principles, concepts and lessons shared throughout the pages of this book cut across all sizes of organizations, from 5 employees to 500 employees to 5,000 employees – the people-centered innovation principles will remain. The innovation principles, concepts and lessons shared throughout the pages of this book cut across all industries and sectors – the people-centered innovation principles will remain. The innovation principles, concepts and lessons shared throughout the pages of this book cut across profit or non-profit, public or private – the people-centered innovation principles will remain. A mentor of mine once said, "if you work the principles, the principles always work." This, most assuredly, is true when applied to the people-centered innovation concepts that will be unpacked in the following pages.

Chapter 2

Innovation

Innovation has long been recognized as an important driver of business growth, economic growth, and profitability for organizations and individuals alike. Innovation is an important ingredient in generating the competitive advantage and long-term growth affecting an organization's development and sustainability. Organizations must meet the challenges of a competitive and globalized 21st century if they want to develop sustainability. Without innovation in an organization, the organization will become obsolete and will eventually be passed by its competitors. So, in response, successful organizations must develop, sustain, and communicate constant innovation throughout their organizations if they want to maintain (or acquire) their position as an industry leader, and earn the moniker of industry disruptor.

What is Innovation anyway?

Innovation has been defined and conceptualized in many ways over the years. In the 80's and 90's many researchers began to define innovation and its component factors. And the decades that followed continued to expand on the previous work. Based on my extensive review of the popular definitions that were sprinkled through the innovation research during the past three decades, I define innovation as: the process of generating, developing and implementing new and creative ideas within systems, technologies, processes, products, procedures, or services that lead to some level of practical and valuable transformation.

"Innovation is: the process of generating, developing and implementing new and creative ideas within systems, technologies, processes, products, procedures, or services that lead to some level of practical and valuable transformation."

Innovation is a beautiful blend of complex and multidimensional activities within an organization. Notice, innovation is not just about ideas, but about ideas being acted upon and implemented within systems, technologies, processes, products, procedures, and services. Innovation is not a clean and linear process, however. It is a creative, non-linear combination of integral ingredients and essential organizational and human factors (the focus of this book) that lead to some level of practical and valuable transformation. Also, it is important to note that innovation is almost always iterative – the outputs of early innovation activities of an organization become the new inputs for later innovation activities within that organization. This non-linear, interconnected, dynamic, and iterative nature characterizes the process and the value of innovation. In the same vein, innovation is not synonymous with invention and it is not synonymous with improvement. There are subtle distinctions. Innovation diverges from invention in that innovation refers to the generation and implementation of a better or more novel idea or method, whereas invention refers more directly to the creation of the method itself. Innovation diverges from improvement in that innovation refers to the notion of doing something different rather than doing the same thing better. Invention and improvement may, in fact, stem from innovation; and innovation may result from invention and improvement.

In short, remember that innovation comes in many sizes, flavors and shapes. It's not just about high-tech advances, which is what typically comes to mind for many people. But, according to our definition, innovation is also about transformation in process, revolutions in products and services, and metamorphosis in systems and procedures.

Quick Case Study

I once led a team of staff through a multi-year organizational transformation. It was a time of scarce resources within the organization and all business units were being thoroughly reviewed to ensure they were bringing about the required return on the investment. I was brought into the organization because it was found to be lacking in return on investment in both financial return and community impact. Over a three-year period the division expended almost $13,000,000 and produced collective gross revenues around $5,000,000 -- that is a loss of nearly $8,000,000. This financial fact, alone, brought this business unit under scrutiny. Adding to the complexity of this financial challenge was the fact that very few within the organization seemed to be alarmed by the financial disparity. My personal experience tells me, and scholarly research supports, that complacency kills innovation within an organization, and makes an organization blind to needed change.

Corey Pruitt

In John Kotter's book, Leading Change, he shares a number of sources of complacency. Some of them that kill innovation within an organization are:

- Too many visible resources
- Low overall performance standards
- Organizational structures that focus employees on narrow functional goals instead of broad business performance
- A lack of sufficient performance feedback from external sources
- A kill-the-messenger-of-bad-news culture
- Human nature's capacity for denial when people are already busy or stressed

The result was the accumulation of the following changes that needed to occur through provoking radical people-centered innovation: changes in operational structure, changes in operational processes, changes in products, changes in financial allocations, and changes in focus.

"Complacency kills innovation and makes an organization blind to needed changes."

In the two-year time frame, the organization moved through various people-centered innovation exercises which produced the ripe cultural environment for generating, developing and implementing new and creative ideas within the systems, technologies, processes, products, procedures, and services that led to various levels of practical and valuable transformation. In the end, the organization became not only sustainable, but profitable.

Why Now?

The concept and practice of innovation has been around for a long time, so, why the focus on innovation now? Innovation has never been more important than it is today due to the nexus of the knowledge age in which we currently work and live and the technological advancements that exist. Additionally, innovation is important to focus on because it has many benefits for your organization. Benefits related to revenue, employee engagement, employee retention, community impact, industry transformation, and the list goes on. The benefits of innovation are cyclical in nature. Innovation has a cyclical benefit to organizations and industries as innovation leads to valuable and practical transformation, which leads to revenue growth and/or revenue diversification, which leads to industry and community advancements, which then stimulates more innovation. So, not only does focusing on innovation impact your organization, but also your overall industry.

Have you ever noticed how certain companies within every industry seem to rise to the top as "innovators" within that industry? Ever notice how those innovation-dominant companies seem to continue to come out with "new" and "creative" systems, processes, products, procedures, or services? That is because of this cyclical benefit of innovation.

"Innovation is the application of new solutions that meet new requirements."

Unknown

Radical people-centered innovation, fed by creativity, information, knowledge, and other intangibles now power organizational and economic prosperity. Radical people-centered innovation is the new currency of high-performance work organizations and the new keys to consistent competitive advantage.

Spark: Provoking Radical People-Centered Innovation

All the tangibles and intangibles of radical people-centered innovation come together to power the operational and productivity gains, systems and process improvements, and products and services that enhance organizational and economic achievement in the 21st century.

Corey Pruitt

Chapter 3

*The People-Centered
Innovation Atmosphere*

I am often asked, "what makes an organization ripe for innovation?" My answer is short and simple, "two things, its' people and its' leaders." You see, from my experience, an organization's own employees are uniquely positioned to move an organization through the innovation process. An organization's employees are uniquely positioned to understand the intersection of business operations, creative outputs, product development pipelines, community impact, and customer demand. Additionally, research indicates that employees are crucial drivers for innovation within an organization (Agarwal, 2014; Anderson, Potocnick & Zhou, 2014; De Spiegelaere et al., 2012; De Spiegelaere, Van Gyes & Van Hootegem, 2016). The success of many organizations may ultimately be in the hands of the employee-innovators, as they stimulate change within the organization and encourage overall continued competitiveness of the organization. I call this emphasis and approach to innovation as "people-centered innovation." Innovation can occur at many levels within your organization. It can occur at the level of the individual, team, organization, or at more than one of these levels combined. But, ultimately, the people within the organization will spark the innovation, will implement the innovation, will iterate the innovation and will sustain the innovation outcome.

Radical people-centered innovation requires five sparks. These are five things you can immediately do to increase people-centered innovation within your organization no matter your industry, company size, or sector. They are: 1) institutionalize creativity; 2) spotlight the maternity ward mentality; 3) play in the overlap; 4) allow for the meaningful collision of ideas; and 5) ask innovation-sparking questions. Let's unpack each of these.

Spark #1: Institutionalize Creativity

The first people-centered innovation spark is to institutionalize creativity. Any organization that is currently successful, that does not have creativity ingrained in the fabric of their business, should be concerned. Creativity is essential for innovation. The sad truth is that instead of innovating, many organizations hold out until they are forced to innovate. Or, more common, many organizations leave innovation and creativity up to a few select people or a select division of the organization (the research and development division, for example). To institutionalize creativity is to embed it into the fabric of every task, in every person's job, in all departments, at all levels. In other words, creativity is just part of the everyday work at your organization.

Quick Case Study

I was working late one evening and was scribbling on the whiteboard in my office. I was attempting to solve a perplexing operational problem that had been hounding the institution I was working for, for some time. As I was channeling my inner coach and outlining possible "moves" and "plays" with x's and o's on the whiteboard, in walks the gentleman who collected the garbage and cleaned the windows each night. He and I had many conversations over the past few months about his family, his interests, and his future. As he entered the room we did some small talk to catch up. I then pointed to the whiteboard and said, "here are a few options I am looking at to decrease the onboarding time for new hires and still keep the same rigor and information-share…it's not quite there yet, what do you make of all this?" He dumped a small office trash bin and set it down. He walked toward the whiteboard and started to smile. He then proceeded to show me how I could blend two of the options I had penned, as well as to include a series of additional ideas that would drastically streamline the process. Our ideas began to coalesce and just a few minutes later we had cracked the perplexing problem and were able to shift to explore the validity of our collective ideas. Had someone else walked into the room at that moment, they would have never guessed that one person was among the executive team and the other was performing janitorial services. Because, at that moment, we were displaying institutionalized creativity. The great thing about this was, moments like these were not out of the norm for this institution.

So, what is creativity, and how can it become institutionalized? Creativity, as defined by Theresa Amabile, Harvard Professor and well-known creativity researcher, is the production of ideas or outcomes that are both novel and appropriate to some goal or open-ended task. The term novel refers to the idea of original or unexpected, and the term appropriate refers to useful and within resource and task constraints (Sternberg and Lubart, 1999). With this as our backdrop, I expand on Professor Amabile's definition of creativity. Creativity is the ability to surpass traditional ideas, patterns, and norms to create meaningful new ideas or outcomes that are both novel and appropriate to some organizational goal or task.

"Creativity is the ability to surpass traditional ideas, patterns, and norms to create meaningful new ideas or outcomes that are both novel and appropriate to some organizational goal or task."

Your organization already has creative people embedded all throughout. People who already surpass traditional ideas, patterns, and norms. People who already seek to create meaningful new ideas and outcomes. Your goal, then, is twofold: 1) seek out those creative people throughout your organization; and 2) create new creative people throughout your organization.

In seeking out those creative people, how do you know when you have found one? Well, Howard Gardner, creativity and intelligence researcher, explains that creative individuals are characterized by their:

- disposition to convert differences into advantages

- propensity to reflect on their goals

- willingness to analyze their strengths and weaknesses and then leverage their abilities

- ability to frame seeming setbacks or failures as nudges to greater achievement in the future

- aptitude to demonstrate intrapersonal intelligence

- comfort with taking risks and showing perseverance, even in the face of doubt and uncertainty from others

So, you may be able to spot a few creative employees, but how do you create new ones? Dr. Amabile has provided the field of creativity studies with one of the most simple and yet comprehensive frameworks for the topic, and this creativity framework is certainly applicable in your people-centered innovation quest to institutionalize creativity. Creativity arises through the convergence of three influences: knowledge, creative thinking, and intrinsic motivation.

Knowledge:

Within the conversation of creativity, knowledge is all the relevant information that an individual brings to a creative effort. Howard Gardner expands on creative knowledge by concluding there are two types of knowledge that may be required for creativity: in-depth experience and combinatory capability.

1) In-depth experience. This is the longer-term experience and focus in one specific area that allows people to build expertise that serves as a foundation for creativity within a specific domain.

2) Combinatory capability. This is just fancy psychology - speak for the ability to combine previous knowledge with new knowledge, as well as combine seemingly disparate elements in new ways.

Taking into account what Dr. Amabile and Howard Gardner express, perhaps a good knowledge profile for individual creativity within your organization is an individual with a breadth of understanding across multiple domains, and one or two areas of in-depth expertise. Some researchers call this the T-shaped mind. The term 'T-shaped' was first used many years ago by McKinsey & Company to describe the type of person they were looking to hire, then the phrase was popularized by the CEO of design and innovation firm IDEO, Tim Brown. Breadth and depth of knowledge is echoed by other creativity and innovation experts.

Frans Johansson recommends in his book, The Medici Effect, that in order to maximize one's creative potential, one "must strike a balance between depth and breadth of knowledge."

Creative Thinking:

The second element in the creativity framework is creative thinking. Creative thinking relates to how people within your organization approach problems. Dr. Amabile suggests that a few key aspects of creative thinking are:

- Comfort in disagreeing with others and trying solutions that depart from the status quo

- Combining knowledge from previously disparate fields

- Ability to persevere through difficult problems and dry spells

- Ability to step away from an effort and return later with a fresh perspective

It, of course, just makes sense that part of institutionalizing creativity would entail influencing creative thinking.

Intrinsic Motivation:

The third element in the creativity framework is intrinsic motivation. Intrinsic motivation occurs when people are motivated to do something because it brings them pleasure, they think it is important, or they feel that how they are behaving is significant. Intrinsic motivation is generally accepted as key to creative production, and the most important motivators for creativity are intrinsic passion and interest in the work itself. Indeed, many theorists, industrial/organizational psychologists, and business consultants see motivation as the most important component of creativity.

There is so much evidence in favor of intrinsic motivation and its connection to creative outputs that Dr. Amabile has coined the concept, Intrinsic Motivation Principle of Creativity. The Intrinsic Motivation Principle of Creativity is: people will be most creative when they feel motivated primarily by the interest, satisfaction, and challenge of the work itself—and not by external pressures [i.e., extrinsic motivation]."

"Even more than particular cognitive abilities, a set of motivational attributes—childlike curiosity, intrinsic interest, perseverance bordering on obsession—seem to set

individuals who change the culture apart from the rest of humankind."

Jeanne Nakamura & Mihaly Csikszentmihalyi

Institutionalized creativity can be achieved through implementing the following nine creativity-stimulation strategies (clearly, this is not an exhaustive list):

- Provide a sense of positive challenge in the work.

- Allow for collaborative work teams that are diversely skilled and idea-focused.

- Allow for freedom in carrying out the work.

- Ensure leaders at all levels constantly encourage the development of new ideas.

- Ensure senior leadership clearly articulate a creativity-encouraging vision.

- Recognize and reward creative work.

- Identify formal and informal mechanisms for developing, sharing and implementing new ideas.

- Practice the norm of actively sharing ideas across the organization.

- Provide sufficient resources (time and money) for the pursuit of creative efforts.

The creativity of employees can be enhanced by environments or efforts that encourage the individual to generate new variations and new combinations of ideas. To produce institutionalized creativity, these strategies thrive on the influence of leaders at all levels, and the collective buy-in of the employees. I would encourage you to look at your own organization and see which of these are already present. Which need strengthening? Which are not present in your organization's culture and climate? For these strategies to be present in your organization, not only do I encourage you to look at your own organization, but I also encourage you to look at yourself.

"Without creative ideas to feed the innovation pipeline, so they may be promoted and developed, innovation is an engine without any fuel."

L.D. McLean

Here are two quick things you can do to increase creativity in yourself: think creatively and work creatively. Let's briefly look at each of these.

Think Creatively

For you to grow in your individual creativity try on the following creativity sparking ideas:

1) Use a wide range of idea-creation techniques, such as: brainstorming, free drawing, mind mapping, free writing, storyboarding, six hats technique, Delphi technique, etc. If flexing your creativity muscle is new for you, spend some initial minutes googling "creativity techniques" and you will find a host of tools and strategies.

2) Weekly, or daily, spend 10 minutes generating new and worthwhile ideas. Don't get caught up in how radical or incremental the ideas are, just spend time allowing your brain to focus on idea generation.

3) Weekly, give yourself the freedom to refine, analyze, elaborate, and evaluate the ideas you previously generated to improve and maximize your individual creative efforts.

Work Creatively

For you to grow in your individual creativity expand your skillset related to how you work with others:

1) Play with different strategies to effectively communicate new ideas to others in your organization. There are many courses and workshops on communication and even on story telling that you can attend to brush up on these skills.

2) Be open and responsive to new and diverse perspectives from your colleagues and employees.

3) Incorporate group feedback and group input into your work.

4) When working on a team, demonstrate originality and resourcefulness in how you approach your work and how you solve problems.

5) Understand and convey that creativity and innovation is a long-term, iterative process of small successes and frequent mistakes.

6) Shift your view and your language around "failure". Shift from "failure" to "an opportunity to learn".

The first people-centered innovation spark is: institutionalize creativity. You spent a few minutes uncovering what institutionalized creativity means, what it takes to spark it, and how you can personally influence and enhance creativity in yourself and others. Now shift and look at the second people-centered innovation spark: spotlight the maternity ward mentality.

Spark #2: Spotlight the Maternity Ward Mentality

Years ago, I led a series of training workshops for doctors and nurses related to communication skills and health behavior change strategies they could use with their patients. Often, the training was conducted at the various hospitals, and while there, I always liked to tour the hospital and see the various areas. The tour would inevitably include areas ranging from the emergency room, to the intensive care unit, and on to the maternity wing of the hospital. Two of my favorite places to tour were the emergency room (ER) and the maternity ward. The reason, many businesses operate like one of these two hospital areas.

Many businesses and organizational units operate like an emergency room. They are great at dealing with the daily emergencies of their business. Great with diagnosing corporate ailments. Great with fielding issues and putting out the proverbial fires. But, these businesses rarely focus on issues like employee engagement, building culture, and sparking radical people-centered innovation. Additionally, emergency rooms don't fully take into consideration all of the issues that caused a patient to be there. They treat the current issue. Similarly, some organizations don't take into consideration how they got into their current situation.

On the flipside, there are some businesses and organizations that operate like a maternity ward. They focus on incubating and nurturing new ideas, new processes, and new products. They focus on the details of how consumers and customers experience their products and services, and how to continually make it better. The businesses that have the maternity ward mentality focus not only on intra-organizational collaborating (like the collaboration it takes to ensure a healthy delivery in the maternity ward), but also on dedicated internal and external support structures for innovation.

People-centered innovation is fueled by spotlighting the maternity ward mentality within your organization. That means, bringing to light the requisite environment, support, mind-frame, belief system, communication processes, and leader sponsorship which creates the nexus where radical people-centered innovation can occur. The maternity ward mentality is not, however, a unit or sub-division within the organization (don't equate this to the Research and Development division of an organization). People-centered innovation and the maternity ward mentality is wholistic and inclusive of all employees. The maternity ward mentality runs from the top of the organization to the bottom of the organization. Yes, an organization needs to deal with daily issues, but when daily emergencies and issues get in the way of innovating for the profitability and sustainability of the organization, then organizational longevity is in jeopardy.

The second people-centered innovation spark is: spotlight the maternity ward mentality. In doing so you shift focus from daily emergencies to incubating and nurturing new ideas, new processes, and new products, which in turn leads to overall organizational profitability and sustainability. Now, look at the third people-centered innovation spark: play in the overlap.

Spark #3: Play in the Overlap

The third people-centered innovation spark is: Play in the overlap. Through my innovation work with organizations and individuals I have found that the concept of innovation is often too big or too broad a concept. So much so, that people say they know what innovation is, but they can't really explain it. I have concluded that many people do not really understand how innovation relates to the larger picture of their organization. So, over the years I have come to relate to the concept of innovation in a very simple and very understandable way. I use a simple Venn diagram to show the overlapping relationship between what is and what ought to be. You see, radical people-centered innovation is the space between what is and what ought to be.

Innovation is two concentric circles in which one circle is labeled "now," the other circle is labeled "future," and in the overlap is where you will find what's next for any business, organization, or industry. It is playing in the overlap where creative ideas, radical solutions to problems, groundbreaking strategies, and revolutionary systems are incubated.

When people in your organization are allowed to, better yet -- encouraged to play in the overlap, then a new currency of success is born within your organization. That new currency of success is creativity, ingenuity, originality, and resourcefulness. When people in your organization play in the overlap, solving important organizational challenges (massive challenges and minor challenges) is what matters most. And, it matters most because of the overarching impact it has on the organization, the community, and consumers it serves.

Quick Case Study

I once had the pleasure of assisting a division of an organization through a major change. Throughout the change, the vision I had to cast was one that noted and acknowledged the current state of the organization, the transition state, and the future state. In acknowledging the current state – and the fact that employees were comfortable with and preferred the current state – I had to carefully communicate that this is the place from which we will be leaving because the future state was painted in such a way that it was both imaginable and attainable. But, in order to successfully transition into the future state, they needed to play in the overlap. They needed to know that it was acceptable to play in the overlap. They needed to constantly hear that it was encouraged to play in the overlap. They needed constant communication that innovation was the only way they would ever achieve the future state. In time, that division did push through to the future state. They innovated in almost every way imaginable. They innovated in product, process, systems, technology, procedures, and operationally.

"Accepting a vision of the future can be a challenging intellectual and emotional task…letting go of the status quo, coming to grips with the sacrifices, coming to trust others is the really hard part of the vision acceptance process."

John Kotter

So, how do you successfully play in the overlap? Here are three steps you can take to encourage your team or organization to play in the overlap:

1) Communicate the current state - express that the chief goal is to clarify which problems you're going to solve,

why they are important to solve, and for whom you are solving them.

2) Communicate the future state – that is vividly painting the vision of the desired future and how innovating in the problem area(s) will bring "xyz" benefits and have "xyz" outcomes. (*insert your own benefits and outcomes where I have placed "xyz"*).

3) Communicate the power of playing in the overlap – that is, continually encourage your employees to spend time in this place. Often, the overlap is uncomfortable, itchy, and unknown, which can lead to stress for some employees. So, the more you encourage them to spend time playing in the overlap, the more effective they will be in that space.

Encouraging your team or organization to play in the overlap has a lot to do with communication. Large portions of the innovation research agree with the notion that leadership communication plays an active role in innovation creation because leadership communication skills are responsible for influencing employees' motivation, commitment, and performance within the organization (Crowley, 2011; Groysberg & Slind, 2012; Kouzes & Posner, 2012; Mautz, 2015; Mayfield & Mayfield, 2002). So, don't take your innovation communication lightly when it comes to playing in the overlap.

The third people-centered innovation spark is: play in the overlap. Playing in the overlap is the space between what is and what ought to be, and it is the space where innovation is incubated. Now, take a look at the fourth people-centered innovation spark: allow for meaningful collisions of ideas.

Spark #4: Allow for Meaningful Collisions of Ideas

The fourth people-centered innovation spark is: allow for meaningful collisions of ideas. Recall that our definition of innovation is "the process of generating, developing and implementing new and creative ideas within systems, technologies, processes, products, procedures, or services that lead to some level of practical and valuable transformation." Within this definition is the inherent two-pronged foundation upon which innovation sits: generating ideas and implementing ideas. Notice the constant – ideas! We can agree that ideas are born, nurtured and developed in many ways. One of the most powerful moments, however, in the idea generation phase of innovation is when multiple ideas collide. It is in that moment, when ideas mash, bump, infuse, knock, marinate, and collide, that makes for meaningful and momentous innovation. Some researchers call this collision moment a cross-pollination of ideas.

The reason meaningful collisions of ideas are so important to innovation is because innovation is about collective intelligence. It is a team sport. It requires excellent collaboration among siloed business and functional units and across geographies. The meaningful collisions of ideas is about finding the best ideas inside and outside your organization and combining them, which is a hallmark of successful people-centered innovation. The meaningful collisions of ideas are so important because collective intelligence will eat individual intelligence for breakfast any day.

"Collective intelligence will eat individual intelligence for breakfast any day."

Quick Case Study

One of the divisions that I led had amazing collective intelligence, and was ripe for opportunity for a meaningful collision of ideas. So, I hosted an innovation pitch challenge. I proposed three projects and allowed all the employees in the division to select one of the projects that they wanted to be a part of, forming a project team. The projects ranged from an internal process improvement, to a customer experience, to internal vendor experience. They placed their name on a sticky note, with two to three aspects about themselves that they would bring to the mini-team that would be tackling that project. We gave them 30 days to collectively ideate, create, design and develop something innovative related to each project. After 30 days the teams came back and presented their innovation project to the rest of the team. We hyped up the pitch competition by getting a little innovation trophy (in the shape of a light bulb) and some Starbucks gift cards. We had all members of the division evaluate the innovation pitch on a few criteria: a) "cool" factor, b) "creative" factor, c) "ease of implementation" factor, and d) time to "go live" factor. Each factor used an abbreviated Likert scale. Note: in no way was the evaluation touted as being a validated instrument. It was meant to be a fun and engaging way for co-workers to interact around other co-workers' ideas. As leadership, we presented the innovation trophy to the team that was collectively evaluated the highest. We eventually, then, implemented each of the three innovations that were presented. This innovation challenge was successful because it afforded the opportunity for employees from various focus areas the freedom to allow their ideas to collide.

So, how do you successfully allow for the meaningful collision of ideas within your organization? Here are three tips you can use to allow for the meaningful collision of ideas in your organization:

1) Create collision opportunities – meaningful collisions of ideas are established when leaders, at all levels of the organization, create collision opportunities for their employees. For example, take the innovation pitch challenge that was shared in the Quick Case Study. This is just one example. Other companies have created collision opportunities through: 1) Jam Sessions - gather two to three representatives from each department, put them in a room for 2 hours and give them a perplexing challenge that your company faces. The goal, two to three options to solve the perplexing challenge by the end of two hours; 2) Think-Pair-Share (shamelessly stolen from the education arena) - you share a vision of a future state with regard to a particular product, process, procedure, etc. Then you have individuals come up with ideas on their own. Next you pair individuals and have them either combine their individual ideas, or come up with a new collective idea. Lastly, the pairs share their work with the larger group. The larger group can select one (or more) of the

collective ideas, or the larger group can form a new idea by mashing ideas from the pairs. There are, of course, many ways to create collision opportunities. Go wild!

2) Create collision spaces – Sometimes, what is needed is a place for ideas to collide. This can take the form of a collaboration space outfitted with dry-erase boards, dry-erase table tops, projection and computer hook ups, reconfigurable table settings, etc. or, It can even take the form of a casual collaboration space with couches and coffee tables, or any other configuration where your intent is to bring people together and have them interact around a topic, concept, challenge, etc. It is not as much about the "stuff" that is available, as it is about the act of engaging and collaborating. I can already hear it now, "but, our organization is spread across locations, states, countries…" Don't let that stop you from creating collision spaces. Many companies use virtual meeting software that often has collaborative features such as virtual whiteboards, breakout spaces, chat boards and discussion forums. Take full advantage of

the technology that is available to collaborate long distance.

3) Create collision language – The last tip to allow for the meaningful collisions of ideas is to create collision language. In short, be sure your language (as a people-leader) is sprinkled with encouragement to collide around ideas. For example, "That is an interesting idea, you should totally collide this idea with what Aiden is doing around systems integration." "Angela, I think you are really on to something. If you are willing to collide this idea with Adyson, I have a hunch the two of you will come up with something really amazing." "There is room for some innovation related to this. Zach and Riley, I would love if the two of you collided on this and see what comes up." Of course, there are a million and one ways to encourage the meaningful collision of ideas within your employees. Try it on for size and see how it most naturally flows from your mouth.

The fourth people-centered innovation spark is: allow for meaningful collisions of ideas. When it comes to innovation, one of the most powerful moments is the idea generation phase when multiple ideas collide. It is in that moment of collision that the next level of what could be becomes a reality. Now, take a look at the fifth and final people-centered innovation spark: ask innovation-sparking questions.

"When it comes to innovation, one of the most powerful moments is the idea generation phase when multiple ideas collide. It is in that moment of collision that the next level of what could be becomes a reality."

Spark #5: Ask Innovation-Sparking Questions

The last people-centered innovation spark is: ask innovation-sparking questions. Recall how we define innovation: the process of generating, developing and implementing new and creative ideas within systems, technologies, processes, products, procedures, or services that lead to some level of practical and valuable transformation. The front end of the innovation process is so important, that this people-centered spark is all about feeding the innovation beast.

In all sales organizations that I have had the pleasure to work with, one thing comes quickly into focus. That is, the amount of effort that is put into feeding the front end of the sales pipeline has a direct impact on the quality of the outputs at the back end of the sales pipeline. Well, the same is true with innovation. The more time an organization spends feeding the front end of the innovation idea pipeline, directly impacts the quality and quantity of the outputs at the back end of the innovation pipeline. The good news is, the people-centered innovation spark of "ask innovation-sparking questions" is the shortest route to feeding the innovation idea pipeline.

"The more time an organization spends feeding the front end of the innovation idea pipeline, directly impacts the quality and quantity of the outputs at the back end of the innovation pipeline."

In my book, "Action From Interaction: The art and science of performance communication" I shared the power and benefits of asking question. Questions are powerful because:

- They provide the opportunity to think and process.
- They invite one to express themselves more fully.
- They develop a dialogue and conversation.
- They elicit details.
- They uncover opinions, knowledge, feelings, thoughts and issues.

Talking about questions often sparks additional questions (yes, I understand the irony in what I just said). You may have some of these questions currently swirling around in your mind: What types of questions do I ask? What makes a question an innovation-sparking question? Who should be doing the asking? Who should be doing the answering? Let's spend a moment to respond to these common questions about innovation-sparking questions, and just for fun let's answer them in reverse order.

Question: *Who should be doing the answering?*

Answer: There are a few options here. Some organizations have all their staff answer innovation-sparking questions. Some organizations split their questions among particular divisions, so as to make sure that not only one division is considered the "innovators" within the company. Other organizations start with an exercise in having their senior leadership (or some variation of leadership levels) respond to innovation-sparking questions. In short, it depends on your organization. But, I would highly suggest the following, related to who should be doing the answering.

1) Have diversity in thought/opinion – this allows for diversity in ideas and not just a group of "yes-men" and "yes-women".

2) Have diversity in hierarchy/levels/bands – this allows for a deeper and richer perspective on what problems or challenges upon which to focus innovation efforts,

as well as a host of other benefits because of the knowledge and expertise each person brings to the group. This essentially means, be sure you have representation from all levels in the organization.

3) Have diversity in divisions/departments – as we have alluded to before, the meaningful collision of ideas increases exponentially when there is cross-division and cross-department diversity. There is something to be said when an engineer, an accountant and a social media expert mash their ideas together in response to an innovation-sparking question.

4) Have diversity in culture – there is such a richness that is added to the response of innovation-sparking questions when there are multiple cultures all responding to the same question. Our individual cultures influence so much of how we behave, what we think, and what we believe. Having a diversity in culture allows those various behaviors, thoughts and beliefs to influence the way in which we respond to the innovation-sparking questions being asked.

Question: Who should be doing the asking?

Answer: This is a short and simple answer. Leadership at all levels. There are many interesting studies that conclude leadership (consisting of managers, supervisors, directors, vice presidents, presidents, chiefs, etc.) has the unique capacity and position to motivate innovative activities within their employees (Manso, 2011). Another study by Mayfield and Mayfield (2004), deduced that there is a significant link between leader communication and worker innovation. So, you can see it is of vast importance who is asking the innovation-sparking questions. (Side benefit: there is a side benefit for leaders to be the askers - recall the discussion on the people-centered innovation spark, "institutionalize creativity" - the first people-centered innovation spark. That is, innovation culture thrives on the influence of leaders at all levels).

Question: What makes a question an innovation-sparking question?

Answer: An innovation-sparking question is any question which instigates and activates idea generation within the innovation process. That means, you have at your disposal endless questions you can ask. But, wait, don't get overwhelmed by the possibilities. First, take a look at the next question and answer.

Question: *What types of questions do I ask?*

Answer: I am glad you asked, as that is the purpose of the remainder of this book. By the time you get through chapters six and seven you will be equipped with the right innovation-sparking questions to ask. But, first, let's get you started with question training through two powerful questions.

Question asking training wheels

When my children were little, they had training wheels on their bicycles. These training wheels, as you may recall, allowed for the bike rider to slowly and safely learn how to balance on two wheels ,while knowing they had the support of the training wheels which were attached to the back tire of the bike. As we grow up there are, in fact, many other times in which this concept of training wheels impacts our learning curve. Think about a time when you were new to a position at work. You most likely received some kind of onboarding training – that is "training wheels" in action. Think about a time when you downloaded a new app on your smartphone, you most likely had a quick tutorial of what the bells, whistles, and clicks do – that is "training wheels" in action. Asking innovation-sparking questions, also requires a short bit of "training wheels." Here are two seemingly simple, but very powerful innovation-sparking question stems:

Question 1: Wouldn't it be cool if _____ ? Wouldn't it be cool if we could improve on "xyz" process? Wouldn't it be cool if we were able to serve our customers in "xyz" fashion? Wouldn't it be cool if our consumers could experience "xyz" when they interacted with our product/service? Wouldn't it be cool if "xyz" policy allowed for "xyz" to happen? Etc…etc.

Question 2: Wouldn't it stink if _____ ? Wouldn't it stink if our company was no longer able to produce "xyz" in this way, what would we do next? Wouldn't it stink if we no longer had "xyz" funding to support this initiative, what would we do then? Wouldn't it stink if "xyz" constraint was put into place, how would we handle that? Etc…etc.

Reason these two question stems are powerful:

I get it, these don't seem like "powerful" question stems. But, don't be fooled by their modesty. These question stems are seeds of innovation disguised in simplicity. The power behind these question stems lies in the fact that they 1) spark the creative process that marks the front end of the innovation process; 2) identify important problems and opportunities within an organization; 3) gather necessary information; 4) generate new ideas; and 5), explore the validity of those ideas. In short, these two question stems can become the spark toward Innovation that your organization needs.

"Questions are seeds of innovation disguised in simplicity."

But, just asking and answering questions like these is not the hard part. It's the space between asking questions like these and answering questions like these that is the tricky part. You see, it's within the space of asking and answering questions that you sabotage yourself and your colleagues, in your potential progress (more to come on this brain/innovation sabotage). It is between the act of asking and answering that your mind frantically tries to ground yourself back into your current reality and pushes away anything that smells like change. It is between the act of asking and answering that your brain does a phenomenal job at finding all the reasons why you can't do something, all the ways in which you are lacking resources, all the reasons why you should just stop now. So, as you go about the business of asking and answering innovation-sparking questions, take caution to not be arrested by the unconstructive and pessimistic brain blocks that are lurking in the space between asking and answering.

Now that you have covered the five people-centered innovation sparks: 1) institutionalize creativity; 2) spotlight the maternity ward mentality; 3) play in the overlap; 4) allow for meaningful collisions of ideas; 5) ask innovation-sparking questions; shift gears for a bit and focus on some impairments to innovation. The impairments you will focus on do not reside between the walls of the organization, rather they reside between the ears of you and your employees. Take a look.

Corey Pruitt

Chapter 4

The Sabotaged Brain

A politician, an athlete and a priest walk into a coffee shop… sounds like the start to a bad joke, doesn't it? What comes to your mind when you hear the word "politician?" What mental references get stirred up when you hear the word "athlete?" What mental images emerge from the word "priest?" What mental framework do you have around the word "coffee shop?" Everyone can quickly mentally articulate what these people and places look like in their mind's eye. What if I used a different set of words: cutting-edge, breakthrough, revolutionary, innovative - these words conjure up unique mental frameworks in everyone's mind, as well.

Now, pair this concept of mental framework with the fact that your brain is wired to help you function more efficiently in your perpetually evolving world, especially in the decision-laden space in which you work and conduct business. Your brain contains about 10 billion nerve cells, or neurons. The brain's network of neurons forms a massive information processing system. The brain is an amazing tool, this cannot be disputed. But, did you know some of the efficiencies of the brain are also the very same impediments that are restricting your ability to create the next iteration of innovation and positive disruption for your organization? Take a look at 8 Brain

Blocks that may be sabotaging your ability to generate, develop and implement new and creative ideas within the systems, technologies, processes, products, procedures, or services of your organization.

Brain Block #1: Incessant Drip (Habituation)

What is it: Have you ever had a leaky faucet? At first you hear every single incessant drip, but as time goes on the drip begins to fade into the background. Or, take for example, people who live around airports. At first, they hear every single airplane that is flying overhead, taking off and landing. But, over time, the noise fades into the background where eventually they no longer hear it (until someone brings it to their awareness again). In the field of psychology, the term is called habituation. Habituation refers to the brains' tendency to stop attending to constant and unchanging information in our environment. This feature is actually very useful for your brain, as it allows your brain to filter out information and stimuli so as not to use up your mental energy on things that are constant and unchanging in your work and lives.

How it hinders: So, what's so bad about this? If your brain is, by default, filtering out information, essentially it is telling you that you should be accustomed to something and therefore do not need to fix it or change it. In the corporate world, this filtered familiarity should be thought of as the kiss of death. Essentially, your brain is telling you, you are so familiar with the problem that you no longer see it as a problem. You have, by default, become less responsive. Often, many organizations have developed "work arounds" for problems they have encountered. Those work arounds, over time, become the "new process," and eventually the "problem" or "issue" fades into the background without ever really being fixed or innovated in some way. This is due to the incessant drip phenomenon (habituation). So, what are some tell-tale signs that incessant drip has set in? Here are a few phrases that you, or people in your organization use that are quick signs incessant drip is present:

1) "We have always done it that way."

2) "This is the work-around for _____ ."

3) "We placed a temporary band-aid on that problem/issue."

4) "You just don't understand how we do things around here."

5) "We have been successful doing it this way."

Incessant drip, the brains' tendency to stop attending to constant and unchanging information in our environment, is the first brain block which potentially can sabotage your ability to generate, develop and implement new and creative ideas within your organization.

Brain Block #2: Convenient Accessibility (Availability Heuristic)

What is it: Convenient accessibility is a cognitive "rule of thumb" that suggests you make decisions and judgments based on information that more readily comes to mind. In the field of psychology, it is known as the availability heuristic. Expressed another way, convenient accessibility is the notion that you base your decisions and judgments on how easy it is to retrieve information about an issue from memory, and/or based on the amount of information that readily comes to mind about the particular issue. In essence, your brain says, the easier it is to bring information to mind, the greater its impact on subsequent judgments or decisions.

I travel a lot in my line of work, and I often meet people at airports who fear for their safety traveling in airplanes more than traveling in cars, even though the chances of being in an auto accident are hundreds of times more likely than being in an airplane crash. This is an example of convenient accessibility – feelings and fears based on recent happenings in the community or world. Additionally, convenient accessibility plays a role in other interesting ways. When asked in social surveys, people typically overestimate murder as a major cause of death, and underestimate more common but more frequent causes of death, such as heart disease and stroke.

The brain block of convenient accessibility tells you that because of the frequency that murder and other dramatic causes of death are presented in the mass media, these instances are easier for your brain to retrieve from memory, than are various natural causes of death (heart disease, stroke, diabetes, etc.) which are rarely presented in the media.

How it hinders: While the brains' use of convenient accessibility makes sense a lot of the time, this "ease of retrieval" effect may mislead you. When you falsely assume that because such information is readily available in memory, it is an accurate representation, when, in fact, it might not be accurate. Apply this to your organization, and you can see how convenient accessibility can lead an organization down a path where innovation is not present. When convenient accessibility inaccurately leads leadership to believe that their product is superior in every way over the competition – then innovation conversations don't take place. When convenient accessibility inaccurately leads leadership to believe that their technology can't be rivaled – then innovation-inducing questions don't get asked. When convenient accessibility inaccurately leads leadership to believe that their proprietary processes and procedures are unparalleled – then innovative ideas don't get expressed in meetings.

So, what are some tell-tale signs that convenient accessibility has set in? Here are a few signs that you, or people in your organization, can use to note if convenient accessibility is present:

1) The same corporate "rally cry" has been around for a few years.

2) There is little talk about what competitors are doing in the space.

3) Strategic plans are not updated, or managed, year after year.

4) Decisions and judgements are unilateral with little input from others.

5) Groupthink is present. Note: groupthink is a term coined by social psychologist Irving Janis (1972), that denotes the consensus of opinion of a group without critical reasoning or evaluation of consequences or alternatives.

Convenient accessibility, the brains' tendency to base decisions and judgments on how easy it is to retrieve information about an issue from memory, and/or based on the amount of information that readily comes to mind about the particular issue. This is the second brain block which potentially can sabotage your ability to generate, develop and implement new and creative ideas within your organization.

Brain Block #3: Option Obstruction (Attentional Bias)

What is it: Option obstruction is the tendency for people's perception to be affected by their recurring thoughts at the time. In other words, it's the brains' tendency to pay attention to some things (called stimuli or sensory cues) while simultaneously ignoring others. In psychology terms this is called attentional bias. Option obstruction can often influence how you remember events, as well as how you recall events in your life. For example, have you noticed how certain people in your meetings tend to surface similar solutions for different problems that the organization faces? Option obstruction tells us that people who frequently think of only one particular pool of solutions pay more attention to the information that confirms that single pool of solutions, and typically don't venture too far outside of that pool.

How it hinders: When you are trying to make an important decision or come up with breakthrough ideas, option obstruction is a brain block that does not let you consider all of the possibilities. While we might think we take all the options into consideration, the reality is we often skip over some alternatives and possible outcomes. In some cases, our attention becomes focused on just a few of the options while we ignore the rest. You can quickly see how the option obstruction phenomena can lead to poor decision-making and lack of creative solutions, as you already have a bias towards one mental stimulus and may more likely base your decisions on that preference. This failure to consider alternative possibilities could lead you and your organization toward a poor sense of judgment and decision making, and away from innovation-inducing thoughts, behaviors and solutions.

So, what are some tell-tale signs that option obstruction has set in? Here are a few signs that you, or people in your organization, can use to note if option obstruction is present:

1) Solutions to problems and issues are typically a one-size-fits-all approach.

2) There is an unnerving death grip on historic processes, methods and systems.

3) There is little cross-pollination of ideas and solutions when problems arise.

Option obstruction is the tendency for your perception to be affected by your recurring thoughts at the time, influencing your inability to consider alternative possibilities, as specific thoughts guide your train of thought in a certain, and often unchanging, track. Option obstruction is the third brain block which potentially can sabotage your ability to generate, develop and implement new and creative ideas within your organization.

Brain Block #4: Perceptual Presumptions (Perceptual Expectancy)

What is it: Perceptual presumptions (in psychology terms known as perceptual expectancy) is the tendency to perceive things a certain way, or only notice certain aspects, because your previous expectations influence your perceptions. In other words, your presumptions and expectations shape your experiences by making you especially sensitive to only specific kinds of information. This predisposition to perceive things in a certain way based on expectations and assumptions about the world is often expressed through a simple social psychological demonstration. Participants are provided with a very brief presentation of non-words such as "sael." Participants who were told to expect words about animals read the world "sael" as "seal," but other participants who were expecting boat-related words read the word "sael" as "sail." It was the presumptions that the participants brought with them that influenced their overall perceptions of what they were seeing and experiencing.

Try on another example. Have you ever had one of those days where you are running from one meeting to the next? Literally, back to back to back meetings. If so, you have probably had one of those moments when you totally misunderstood the context of the conversation that was taking place in meeting number two or three. You then asked a question or made a statement to contribute to the meeting, and everyone slowly turns their heads toward you as if to say, "what in the world are you talking about?" This is the lingering effects of perceptual presumptions. You brought into this meeting the presumptions and expectations that were part of the previous meetings. These presumptions and expectations formed the backdrop for your perspective, and it just so happened to be an inaccurate backdrop for the new conversations.

How it hinders: Perceptual presumptions hinders your ability to see the whole picture. So, if you are in the business of finding solutions, seeking new innovations, and generating fresh ideas, you may have difficulty due to the limitations your perceptual presumptions places on your brain.

I once was in a meeting with a group of other executives in a large organization in which I served. The conversation quickly shifted to how the division I was leading could be absorbed into another division, which included a potential move of all my employees into a different location. At least, that was my perception of the meeting. Come to find out, my perception of the meeting was skewed. What was really being expressed as a joke among colleagues was taken seriously by me. Why the misunderstanding?

Perceptual presumptions came into play. For the week prior to this meeting I was in various other meetings in which I heard rumors of my division being absorbed, rumors of people politically positioning themselves to take over, and to all but strip my division of its budget lines. Needless to say, those previous meetings and conversations colored what I heard in this current meeting, how I processed the information and even how I translated the information into conspiracy-laden rhetoric. Which, by the way, is the farthest thing from my normal thought process. A clear indication that perceptual presumptions was at play.

So, what are some tell-tale signs that perceptual presumptions have set in? Here are a few signs that you, or people in your organization, can use to note if the perceptual presumptions phenomena is present:

1) Only one flavor of issue is constantly surfacing (i.e. your organization only has technology issues, or only has system issues, or only has people issues).

2) Only one flavor of questions is being asked (i.e. when seeking solutions your organization is only asking questions around the human impact, or only around technology impact, or only around process impact, but rarely asking multi-dimensional questions that look at all of the various impacts and influences within the organization).

Perceptual presumptions is the tendency to perceive things a certain way because your previous expectations influence your perceptions. Perceptual presumptions is the fourth brain block which potentially can sabotage your ability to generate, develop and implement new and creative ideas within your organization.

Brain Block #5: Functional Fixedness

What is it: Functional fixedness is a block to problem solving that comes from thinking about objects in terms of only their typical functions. Functional fixedness involves thinking about something only in terms of its functionality rather than new ways in which it could be used. Years ago, when consultants were doing a lot of brainstorming work with companies, they all started with the paperclip activity. You may have done this very same activity. You are handed a paperclip and paired with a partner. You and your partner are given five minutes to generate a list of uses for the paperclip, other than its typical use of keeping papers attached to one another. This exercise was an attempt to get folks out of their general fixedness of the functions of a paperclip and to mentally "prime the pump" for application to other ideas within their organizations.

How it hinders: Functional fixedness reveals how you can have mental blocks for various items which only allow you to view or use that item in a particular way (the way it was originally designed). This, then, fixes your attention on that purpose and excludes all other purposes. Many innovations are born out of mashing ideas, concepts, processes, and technologies. Innovations are born out of re-purposing the old into the new, so you can see how this brain block can be a major inhibitor to innovation within your organization.

I once worked within an organization that conducted mental health risk assessments for individuals dealing with suicidal ideations and those who attempted suicide. We met with the patient in the hospital after they were medically released. Each time we met with a patient we had to draft up an assessment report that would then become part of the patients' medical record. The owner of the organization and I would brainstorm ways in which we could streamline this mental health assessment report process. We went through many iterations, using templates, using Microsoft Office Word macros, and various other database ideas. Then, we moved out of our functional fixedness mindset and combined our assessment report with the technology the organization used to capture contact information on their website, an e-forms builder. The e-forms builder allowed the counselor on duty to simply fill in the necessary assessment prompts, and then push a button on the form builder and a report was generated. Then the report was automatically sent to the home office, the attending Physician, and the attending Nurse. This was, of course, prior to some of the current technologies and apps that provide this same type of service today. Just as a point of reference, we also used pagers, so we were way ahead of the innovation curve with this implementation.

Research has shown that as you get older and gain more experience using objects, you lose the functional fluidity and creative opportunities with objects, and instead become fixated on their "proper" use. When faced with a problem or issue, when functional fixedness is present, it would be rare that one would look for what is called "non-related domain inspiration." Non-related domain inspiration is when one would increase the likelihood of generating more creative solutions by considering domains outside of the original representation of the problem or issue at hand. In other words, looking at issues or objects through multiple lenses.

So, what are some tell-tale signs that functional fixedness has set in? Here are a few signs that you, or people in your organization, can use to note if functional fixedness is present:

1) There are no conversations (or only rare conversations) about looking beyond the typical function of a product or process.

2) Questions like, "How else could this work?" and "What are other approaches to solving this problem?" are rarely surfaced.

3) When faced with a problem or issue, it is rare that people within your organization would look for inspiration from non-related domains and only look at domains closely related to the original representation of the problem.

Functional fixedness involves thinking about something only in terms of its functionality rather than new ways in which it could be used. Functional fixedness is the fifth brain block which potentially can sabotage your ability to generate, develop and implement new and creative ideas within your organization.

Brain Block #6: Mental Set

What is it: Your mental set is your tendency to persist in using problem-solving patterns that have worked for you in the past. In other words, a mental set is a framework for thinking about a problem. A mental set involves using something that worked for you in the past to solve a problem which you are presented with now. For example, if you want to use an elevator to go from floor 1 to floor 15, you have a mental set which tells you how to open an elevator door and select a floor number. As a result, you try to push the button next to the elevator door in order to get it open, and subsequently push the button of the floor to which you want to go when you get on the elevator. What you have done here is used an approach that worked for you in the past (i.e. pushing the correct buttons), to open a new elevator door that you have never seen before (i.e. solve a new problem). This, of course, can be a good thing, as this allows you to make quicker decisions and not have to "re-learn" everything all the time. But, there may be a draw back too.

How it hinders: Mental sets can make it easy to solve a class of problems, but attachment to the wrong mental set can inhibit problem-solving and creativity, much along the same lines as functional fixedness described previously. Your brain sometimes defends its mental sets, even if they are incorrect or illogical. Additionally, you are inclined to behave in ways which confirm your mental sets - that is, you seek ways to provide the evidence for the existence of your current mental sets. It can be a vicious trap (you form your mental set and then create additional evidence to fit your mental set – whether it is accurate or not).

So, what are some tell-tale signs that you are being hindered by your mental sets? Here are a few signs that you, or people in your organization, can use to note if your mental sets are hindering your creativity:

1) When faced with a problem or issue, it is rare that people within your organization would look for inspiration from non-related domains and only look at domains closely related to the original representation of the problem.

2) When faced with a problem or issue, people within your organization staunchly defend their position because it has "worked for them in the past".

Mental set is your tendency to persist in using problem-solving patterns that have worked for you in the past. Mental set is the sixth brain block which potentially can sabotage your ability to generate, develop and implement new and creative ideas within your organization.

Brain Block #7: Confirmation Bias

What is it: Confirmation bias is the tendency to search for evidence that fits your beliefs while ignoring any evidence that does not fit those beliefs. This could be seen as an extension to the mental set phenomena previously described. When new information enters your brain, your brain has the tendency to quickly assess whether or not that new information confirms what you already believe. If it does, it is quickly stored in the "this confirms my belief about xyz" file. If the new information does not confirm what you already believe, your brain does an excellent job of discounting the new information and tossing it aside. Of course, this is an oversimplification, but you get the idea. In short, your confirmation bias grows stronger as you invest more time and energy in your current belief, position, or idea - often making you the least objective person to interpret the new information, issue or problem. As the old saying goes, "What you look for is what you will find."

How it hinders: This brain block is fairly simple to see the drawbacks. If you are consistently seeking information that confirms your initial belief (or technically, if your brain is only allowing information that confirms your initial belief to filter through), and are consistently negating information that opposes your initial belief, then you really are not viewing the entire spectrum of possibilities. This, in turn, will limit your ability to solve problems and create innovation.

So, what are some tell-tale signs that you are being hindered by your confirmation bias? Here are a few signs that you, or people in your organization, can use to note if your confirmation biases are hindering your creativity:

1) If you do not have an open atmosphere where information and experimentation is evaluated by everyone, especially those not working directly on the project.

2) Critical views on the working hypothesis to solve current organizational issues is not encouraged or even considered.

3) Before executing a possible solution to an organizational issue, standards for what the outcomes and results should be are not stipulated (standards in support of the suggestion, and standards that disprove the suggestion should be noted - this is an excellent safeguard against bias sneaking into the interpretation of results).

Confirmation bias is the tendency to search for evidence that fits your current beliefs while ignoring any evidence that does not fit those beliefs. Confirmation bias is the seventh brain block which potentially can sabotage your ability to generate, develop and implement new and creative ideas within your organization.

Brain Block #8: Anchoring

What is it: Anchoring is your brains' tendency to rely too heavily on the first piece of information offered, or on one particular trait or piece of information (the "anchor") when making decisions. During decision making, anchoring occurs when you use an initial piece of information to make subsequent judgments. In other words, you tend to overly rely on your anchor (specific information or a specific value) and then you adjust to that value to account for the other elements of the circumstance. Typically, once you have mentally set the anchor, you have a bias toward that value, as all future estimates, arguments, negotiations, and decisions are made in relation to the anchor.

When I was first starting my company, the Chief Operating Officer and I went on a hunt for office space. We looked at three different properties and several office units within each property. I had created an anchor on the monthly cost of the office unit (I had determined in my mind what I felt was reasonable for the size of space we were looking for) and the proximity of the office unit to my house (nothing more than a 10 minute drive seemed reasonable). Whereas my Chief Operating Officer had created an anchor on the amenities that came with the office units and whether or not the unit had an exterior window to allow for natural light. For each of us, we were using those criteria as a basis for evaluating the value of the office units. The problem would have been fully realized if my Chief Operating Officer or I had gone alone, as we would not have taken into account the elements that fell outside of our individual anchors. So, in this case, having multiple minds (each with different anchors) made for a better overall decision-making process.

How it hinders: So what's the big deal about anchoring? Well, once an anchor is set, your brain does two things. One, all other judgments are made by adjusting away from that anchor; and two, there is a bias toward interpreting other information in light of the anchor you have set. Take the office space example - the initial price offered for the office space sets the standard for the rest of the negotiations, this makes all prices lower than the initial price seem more reasonable (even if they are still higher than what one was initially wanting to pay). This brain block hinders because if your anchor is not accurate, your subsequent judgments and decisions will also not be accurate.

So, what are some tell-tale signs that you are being hindered by your anchors? Here are a few signs that you, or people in your organization, can use to note if your anchors are hindering your creativity:

1) The origin of one's differing opinions and ideas related to the decision being made are rarely shared.

2) Decisions are made in isolation with little input from others.

3) Awareness of personal anchors is low or non-existent.

Anchoring is your brains tendency to rely too heavily on early information offered, or on one particular trait or piece of information when making decisions. Anchoring is the eighth brain block which potentially can sabotage your ability to generate, develop and implement new and creative ideas within your organization.

As you can clearly see, these 8 Brain Blocks can put you, your employees, and your organization at a disadvantage when it comes to creative solution discovery and when it comes to organizational change. But, all is not lost, you can also harness the immense power of your brain to stir new insight and uncover breakthroughs in your products, services and processes.

Chapter 5

Innovation Through Submersive Focus

So, what are leaders supposed to do in this evolving and ever-changing landscape that requires constant innovation? What are leaders supposed to do to leap from where they are now to create the next iteration of innovation and positive industry disruption? How are leaders to get their organization to the proverbial "next level"? The answer is direct and succinct. Leaders must embrace radical people-centered innovation and plunge themselves and their organizations into "submersive focus" through asking innovation-sparking questions (ISQ's). Submersive focus is a profound, meaningful and multilayered cerebral focus on an idea or question.

Submersive focus is a profound, meaningful and multilayered cerebral focus on an idea or question.

In the last chapter you read about how the brain can sabotage innovation. Well, submersive focus is, essentially, the concept of using the human brain like a laser focus to come up with new ideas and fresh solutions. This is the secret to idea generation and innovation – instead of scattering your mental efforts in diffused activity, focus brings a single-mindedness of creative purpose. When it comes to your brain, focus and attention have some unique attributes that you must unpack in order to harness this powerful people-centered innovation tool that you and the people you lead possess. Three areas of focus and attention worth unpacking are: 1) focus and attention – a limited resource; 2) focus and attention - task suffering; and 3) focus and attention – selectivity.

Focus and attention – a limited resource

Consider some everyday situations in which focus and attention are important. When you are in a meeting, when you are driving, when you are eating dinner with your family, when you are taking a certification exam, and when you are having a coaching conversation with your direct reports, are just a few examples where focus and attention are important. In each of these examples, there are numerous irrelevant stimuli – the sounds coming from a meeting in an adjacent conference room, the combination of your cell phone notifications going off while changing your radio stations, the distant roar of an airplane flying over your house during dinner or the birds outside the kitchen window, the hardness of the desk seat or the pressure of your clothing on your skin. Focus and attention use a lot of energy to strike out the irrelevant and to concentrate on the relevant.

Every time you focus your attention you use a measurable amount of glucose and other metabolic resources. Neuroscience research suggests that the more you focus on a given task the less effective you will be at the subsequent tasks. This is especially true for high-stakes tasks like decision-making that people-leaders like you do daily. In 1973, Daniel Kahneman proposed that attention is limited in capacity, and that your ability to carry out multiple tasks simultaneously depends, in part, on how much capacity each task requires. Kahneman's "capacity approach" to attention reveals that attention is a limited pool of mental resources. Some tasks (and the cognitive processes they entail) demand few of these mental resources. Others are highly demanding of mental resources and could even deplete your available attention. The more a task requires from your limited pool of available attention, the more mental effort you exert.

In other words, think of your focus like a finite tank of gas during a long trip. The longer you drive on one leg of your trip, the less gas you have for the second leg of your trip – thus causing the need to fill up again. If this is the case, you can quickly see how distractions, while attempting to focus, can take their toll by draining your finite focus tank. Distractions are costly, they use up what is actually a limited supply of attention and focus, and make you far less effective if you need to do deeper thinking work - like answering the demand to innovate, innovate, innovate.

"Focus is a limited resource"

Focus and attention – task suffering

Not only is focus and attention a limited resource, there are other interesting attributes of focus and attention such as task suffering. Focus and attention are important psychological concepts to unpack in order to fully understand how to use the power of submersive focus in your efforts to innovate. When you think about it, at any given moment, your mind is bombarded with information and stimuli that are all competing for your undivided attention. Your brain is consuming, processing, and routing information on a constant basis. I am reminded of a train station with constant incoming and outgoing trains, and numerous railway switches (forcing trains down specific tracks).

Take a moment and reflect on how many decisions you make during a given work day, and how much information your brain has to process in order to make those decisions. Sometimes, you are conscious of the internal and external information that is coming in moment by moment. And, at other times, you barely notice it at all. But, you might be saying, "I am a master at multi-tasking. To get to the level I am at, one would have to be a master multi-tasker." The research shows that the efficiency of multi-tasking leans more toward being a myth than a reality, at least when it comes to attention and focus. When you try to do two things at once, typically, one or the other task suffers. Suffering takes the form of either the speed of task completion is longer or the quality of performance is poorer as compared with focusing attention on one task at a time.

To be fair, though, some research does conclude that task suffrage does not always occur. If a task can be performed by rote (meaning with little to no attention paid to it), then it may in theory be possible to perform two tasks in parallel, with no loss of speed or accuracy in either task. However, to fall into this realm, the task must meet a few criteria: a) task has to be relatively simple; b) task has to be heavily practiced; and c) task has to be automatic. On the flip side, when each of the tasks demands attention and substantial cognitive effort, it is clear that trying to perform both of them at the same time is a lost cause.

Focus and attention - selectivity

When it comes to focus and attention, not only do you need to realize that it is a limited resource, and the concept of task suffering, but also the concept of selectivity. To keep up with the high demand to innovate you cannot merely "focus," you must be selective with your focus. I call it utilizing submersive focus. Most cognitive psychologists agree that, when it comes to attention, there is divided attention and selective attention. (Hang with me, here, this crash course in psychology is important to sparking radical people-centered innovation). What has been previously shared related to focus and attention and task suffering falls into the divided attention camp. Divided attention is essentially your brain taking in two or more stimuli and being forced to share your limited cognitive resources. For example, at a noisy networking event or business party, you can carry on a conversation with one person while other people are carrying on conversations all around you in which you can hear and process bits and pieces of the other conversations.

Selective attention (submersive focus) is your ability to perceive a single stimulus of interest while ignoring numerous other stimuli. With selective attention, playing off the previous example, you focus on your conversation with the person in front of you and ignore the rest of the conversations that are happening around you. As a personal example, my wife always laughs at me when I am getting ready to park the car, one of the first things I do is turn down the radio. I do this so I can focus my attention on getting the car in the parking space without hitting the other cars around me (which I believe the others drivers appreciate). Selective attention (submersive focus) allows you to focus on what is important at the moment and to ignore the rest.

Another interesting aspect of focus and attention, as it relates to selectivity, is a cognitive psychology concept known as the "central bottleneck." (For the nerdy research folks like me, check out the iterations this concept has made by Googling central bottleneck of attention, and Broadbent, Treisman and Deutsch). The central bottleneck refers to the way in which our brain deals with multiple task situations. Essentially, our brain deals with them in a series (one at a time) rather than in parallel (all at the same time). In other words, our brain becomes selective and prioritizes, and only deals with one response at a time and delaying a response to the other tasks. Of course, the delay could be seconds, but the selectivity of focus and attention has occurred in that short timeframe.

Focus and attention – so what?

Ok, so you now know that focus and attention draw from a limited pool of resources, you know that when you try to focus on two things at once, typically, one or the other suffers, and you know that in the case of highly demanding attention, selective attention is preferred. But why does this matter to you, and why does this matter in a book on provoking people-centered innovation? The short answer - you can imagine if general focus and attention uses substantial mental resources, then submersive focus with the intent to innovate certainly will require an amplification of mental resources.

But don't close up shop yet, there is actually a fairly prescriptive, and fairly easy, process to tap into the realm of submersive focus so you can create the next iteration of people-centered innovation and positive disruption for your organization. This process is called ISQ – Innovation Sparking Questions. The power of innovation-sparking questions was already alluded to back in chapter three. Turn, now, to reveal the secret system of how to make your brain your creative ally in illuminating solutions and generating groundbreaking revolutionary ideas.

"A mind that is stretched by a new experience can never go back to its old dimensions."

Oliver Wendell Holmes

One reason so few people and business rarely activate their potential innovation greatness is because they never direct their innovation focus. Harry Emerson Fosdick once wrote, "No horse gets anywhere till he's harnessed, no steam or gas drives anything until it's confined, no Niagara ever turned anything into light or power until it's tunneled, no life ever grows great until focused."

Recall the analogy used in chapter three of the emergency room versus the maternity ward where the maternity ward allowed for focus and incubation of ideas. Often, people don't concentrate their focus power on generating a distinct innovation idea or solution. In short, they don't activate submersive focus.

"The suns rays do not burn until brought to a focus."

Alexander Graham Bell

Submersive focus is, essentially, the concept of using the human brain like a laser focus to come up with new ideas and fresh solutions. You see, you are where you are right now because of what you have focused upon. Your company, organization or institution is where it is because of what it focused upon. People and entities are always moving in the direction of their focus. Success, failure, innovation, transformation, revolutionary progress and cutting-edge pioneering are all a result of submersive focus. Motivational speaker and author, Jack Canfield says, "What you think about you bring about." What we focus on, we cultivate. What we focus on, we clarify. What we focus on, we intensify. So, how can you tap into submersive focus without shutting off all other stimuli and locking yourself in a dark room (because that just does not seem like the best solution in the workplace)? The answer – your submersive focus on autopilot.

"What we focus on, we clarify. What we focus on, we intensify."

Submersive Focus on Autopilot (The RAS)

Our brain has an incredible built in system called the reticular activating system (RAS). It is a part of the brain located in the brain stem, and it is believed to play a role in many important and diverse functions, including: controlling sleep, behavioral motivation, sex, breathing, and the beating of the heart. Perhaps the most important function of the RAS as it relates to innovation and submersive focus is its control of consciousness. The RAS controls the ability to consciously focus attention on something. The RAS is like your gatekeeper of which information is let into your conscious mind. The RAS has this great default setting; it has to produce what you ask of it. It's like a filter between your conscious mind and your subconscious mind. It takes instructions from your conscious mind (like "I need to identify the barriers to entry into this market segment") and passes it on to your subconscious mind, which becomes diligent and alert to your request. The Reticular Activating System can be viewed as your built-in innovation solution powerhouse when used to its full potential.

"The RAS is your built-in innovation solution powerhouse."

Here are a few simplified examples of your RAS at work:

- You buy a new car and you'll "suddenly" start seeing more of the same car on the road.

- A pregnant woman will start noticing other pregnant women.

- Learn a new concept and you'll begin to see it in action, or hear others talking about it more often.

- While aimlessly Google searching you "suddenly" find the answer to a problem.

- Your baby's slightest cough or cry will awaken you from a deep sleep.

- You hear a new word for the first time, and you'll begin to hear the word used more often in many settings.

What is happening? Your brain is automatically aroused (by your RAS) because you have indicated that it is now something important to you, and therefore your brain should bring it to your awareness. I have taught psychology courses for many colleges and universities over the years. It is something I really enjoy doing. One way I teach my psychology students about the RAS is I say a phrase like the following, "man, you cannot believe how many electrical outlets are on this campus. They are everywhere. I mean, it feels like I see one every ten feet." Then, during a subsequent class session I will ask them how many began to notice more and more electrical outlets in their classrooms, their dorm rooms, the hallways, the common areas, etc. Almost every hand goes up in the room. So, what was I doing? Was I installing electrical outlets all over campus? Had I previously counted all the electrical outlets and knew there were many of them? No, I had no clue how many electrical outlets were on campus, nor did I really know if there were a lot of them or not. What I was doing was priming their RAS. I was bringing to their awareness something that their brain had already placed on the backburner as not worth focused attention (that is, not until you really need an electrical outlet to charge your phone or tablet).

So, what does all of this RAS psychology stuff have to do with radical people-centered innovation in your organization, or product, or service, or industry? It all has to do with the end goal of putting your brain on submersive focus autopilot. Submersive focus on autopilot is exploiting the RAS brain feature so you can tap into innovation and breakthrough ideas. Essentially, asking your brain to process "innovation requests" in a manner that is effortless, automatic and without your full awareness. Your RAS takes what you focus on and creates a filter for it. It then sifts through the data and the mounds of information, and presents only the pieces that are important to you. Essentially, the RAS programs itself to work in your favor without you consciously doing anything.

Have you ever tried to remember something, it is on the top of your head, but you just cannot recall it? So, you start doing something else, and all of the sudden it "pops" into your mind. This is RAS, or automatic processing at work. In this case you were dimly aware that something was happening behind the scenes. Your brain searched for the answer to the request, and was working on autopilot, until it found the answer. Well, you are going to tap into the same thing to put submersive focus on autopilot for the intention of producing constant innovative ideas.

Submersive Focus Power Tool

It's time for you to hack into this automatic processing brain feature, called the RAS, through one ingenious power tool. This power tool is called innovation-sparking questions (ISQ).

"Submersive focus is the art of disciplined asking of innovation-sparking questions (ISQ)."

Chapter 6

Innovation-Sparking Questions (ISQ) and Submersive Focus

The last few pages you dove deep into the psychology of focus and attention and the reticular activating system (RAS) to set the foundation to hack into this automatic processing brain feature to stimulate innovation within yourself and those you lead. A few years ago, I asked myself what could happen if a business leader focused on answering one innovation-sparking question per week for a year? What would happen if a business leader reflected upon, analyzed, and scrutinized only one ISQ for seven days. All mental resources would begin to focus on answering that single innovation question. The benefits of doing this would be astounding for your company's systems, technologies, processes, products, procedures, and services:

- New and creative ideas will be generated

- Solutions to perplexing problems will be identified

- Previously unseen barriers will become visible

- Organizational insights will be unlocked

- Industry insights will be revealed

- Advancements will be realized

- Improvements will be exposed

Just to name a few benefits.

Recall, in chapter two innovation was defined as: the process of generating, developing and implementing new and creative ideas within systems, technologies, processes, products, procedures, or services that lead to some level of practical and valuable transformation.

So, that is going to be your plan of attack to spark innovation in you and your organization. You will strategically ask one innovation-sparking question per week in order to generate and develop new and creative ideas within systems, technologies, processes, products, procedures, and services. To make this ISQ exercise effective, your goal is to constantly answer the ISQ throughout the week. Don't just land on one response, or your first response. (Recall the eight brain blocks from chapter four, and how your brain may be working against your efforts to innovate). Your goal for the week is to continuously write down the ideas that come to your mind as you allow your mind to dive into submersive focus on the specific ISQ. You can jot them down directly in this book, or order a Spark Journal and collect your innovation ideas. But, recall, this book is about sparking radical people-centered innovation. So, don't go at it alone. I recommend you slice your ISQ exercise in one of a few ways. Here are the two most common ISQ exercise methods organizations, and people I have worked with, are using.

1) *Innovation Leadership Challenge*

Many organizations begin their innovation work at the executive leadership level. They kick off with an innovation spark training that I conduct to orient them on how to use the brain to their advantage to produce innovative ideas, as well as how to avoid the various ways the brain uses to sabotage innovative ideas, as well as a few creativity exercises to prime their brain to think differently about their current situation and current challenges. Then I partner with the leadership team to lead them through their weekly ISQ as well as a quarterly innovation ideation process. During the quarterly innovation ideation process they gather their weekly ISQ responses and they work through the QB-PIC process (question, breakthrough, plan, implement, check.)

2) *Innovation Co-Creation*

Many organizations begin their innovation work by including all of the individuals within the organization. This also has a side benefit of generating a larger quantity of exceptional ideas, as well as increasing employee engagement in the workplace. These organizations kick off with an innovation spark keynote provided to the entire organization. This gets everyone on the same page related to the innovation initiative. Additionally, a 4 hour training is provided to the people-leaders in the organization. This training orients them on how to use the brain to their advantage to produce innovative ideas, how to avoid the various ways the brain can sabotage innovative ideas, as well as a few creativity exercises to prime their brain to think differently about their current situation and current challenges. Then I show the people-leaders how to lead their teams through the weekly ISQ, as well as a quarterly innovation ideation process using the QB-PIC process.

Of course, there are other ways you can slice the ISQ exercise to make it work for you and your organization. I will be the last person to tell you there is only one (or two) right ways to do something. Be creative, but be sure you tackle all 52 innovation-sparking questions to get the maximum return on your time investment. And, be sure you're constantly answering the ISQ throughout the week. Again, don't just land on your first response. Your goal for the week is to continuously write down the ideas that come to your mind as you allow your mind to dive into submersive focus on the specific ISQ.

So, start the clock now, and lock in your first ISQ to activate your radical people-centered innovation engine.

Chapter 7

52 Innovation-Sparking Questions

1.

What will the buying criteria be for our customers 5 years from now?

2.

What constraints are we accepting that are forcing us to work to a lower standard?

3.

What one thing could we do right now to make our product/service ridiculously amazing?

4.

If this problem (insert issue) was actually an opportunity how might we capitalize on it?

5.

What should we stop doing immediately?

6.
Where can we break convention?

7.

What successful thing are we doing today that may be blinding us to new growth opportunities?

8.

What are the rules and assumptions my industry operates under? What if the opposite were true?

9.

In what ways are opportunities to do my very best hindered every day?

10.

What process are we living with that we need to change and why have we not changed it yet?

11.

What can we do today to ensure we are relevant five years from now?

12.

What is one small change we can make immediately that will have a large impact on our business?

13.

What perceived barriers do our customers have of us/our product/our service and how can we break down those barriers?

14.

How can our product/service be used in a new and unexpected way?

15.

What one institutional behavior should we stop doing, starting now?

16.
At our best, what do our customers/consumers experience?

17.

At our worst what do our customers/consumers experience?

18.

What is the customers' journey from desire for our product/service to purchase of our product/service, and how can we streamline/ make that journey easier?

19.

When everyone is doing what we are doing, just like we are doing it, what will we do next?

20.
What hard decision have we been avoiding and why have we been avoiding it?

21.

What desires might our customers have that would push us to our current limits?

22.

How can we add more value to our customers/consumers lives?

23.

What counts in our industry and to our consumers that we are not considering?

24.

If we were to go back in time five years what decisions would we make differently?

25.

What potential trends could make our current business model obsolete?

26.

What current people-practices are negatively impacting our customers' experiences?

27.

What current people-practices are positively impacting our customers' experiences?

28.

What best practice are we adhering to that is no longer really a best practice anymore?

29.
What are we tolerating?

30.
What should we be doing more of?

31.

What should we be doing less of?

32.

What are the things we are doing regularly that do not serve or support our goals/mission?

33.

What would we be trying if we knew we could not fail?

34.
What lessons are hiding in one of our current struggles?

35.

What is our favorite way we
sabotage ourselves and our goals?

36.

If we could make a change immediately, how might things be different?

37.

Suppose we continue as we have been, without changing, what might be the worst thing that might happen?

38.
What is not perfect yet?

39.

What assumptions are we making that are blinding us to new opportunities?

40.

What is everyone thinking, but no one has the courage to say out loud?

41.

What action is the person/company that wants to put us out of business doing right now?

42.

If we started from ground zero what would we do differently?

43.

How can we capitalize differently on our greatest strength?

44.

What are we absolutely, without a doubt, the best at?

45.

What is our #1 complaint and what can we do to fix it this week?

46.

If we completely changed the way we communicated about our product/service, what might we say, and how would that look?

47.

What about our product/service, have we been bragging about for years, that really isn't a selling point anymore?

48.

If we were to make our user / customer experience amazing, what would we do differently from what we are currently doing?

49.

What is one thing we can do every day that will astonish our customers / consumers that no one else is doing?

50.

If an outsider jumped into our market, what would they do first to set themselves apart to take away our customers?

51.

What one piece of company legacy - knowledge is hindering our innovation behaviors...and how can we change it?

52.

What other questions should we be asking that we are not asking?

Corey Pruitt

Chapter 8

What Now?

Well, you have now traveled through an extensive exercise that exemplified radical people-centered innovation. You have traveled through 52 innovation-sparking questions. You have, no doubt, uncovered some new ideas, saw organizational problems and challenges from new perspectives, and generated countless innovative ideas. One thing you may have noticed is that there is a connection between the quality of creative output and sheer quantity. The more people-centered innovation ideas you, your team, and colleagues produce, the more likely your organization is to discover innovation success. Dr. Simonton, a creativity researcher out of UC Davis, explains one can conclude with great confidence that creative output is linked to the amount of time a person is actively engaged in a creative domain. In my research I found an interesting article that was first published in Research Technology Magazine, in 1997 titled "3,000 raw ideas = 1 commercial success!" Authors Stevens and Burley summarized a study whereby they reviewed things such as patent literature, venture capitalist experience, project literature, etc., and they concluded that "across most industries, it appears to require 3,000 raw ideas to produce one substantially new, commercially successful industrial product." Of course, your goal throughout the ISQ exercise was not just to produce a commercially viable product, but it is fascinating to see how the ideas funnel. The researchers continued by noting the idea funnel broke out by the following:

- 3,000 raw ideas turn into 300 ideas for which minimal action is taken

- 125 of the 300 ideas become small projects

- 9 out of the 125 become significant projects with a significant development effort

- 4 out of the 9 become major development efforts

- 1.7 out of the 4 is commercially launched

- 1 out of the 1.7 launched (59%) becomes commercially successful

This study would need to be completed again to see how viable the data is today, but nonetheless, lessons can still be gleaned from this research. The primary lesson being, more innovative ideas will equate to a higher probability that innovation and change will occur in your organization. Radical people-centered innovation is a beautiful blend of complex and multidimensional activities by the people within an organization. Innovation is not just about ideas, but about ideas being acted upon and implemented. Radical people-centered innovation is a creative, non-linear combination of integral ingredients and essential organizational and human factors. Also, it is important to remember that innovation is almost always iterative – the outputs of early innovation activities become the new inputs for later innovation activities.

Well, your journey to radical people-centered innovation is coming to a close. So, spend a few moments to recap the important aspects that were unpacked throughout these pages. Review the definition of innovation, the five sparks of a people-centered innovation atmosphere, and the 8 Brain Blocks to innovation.

Recall, the definition of innovation is: the process of generating, developing and implementing new and creative ideas within systems, technologies, processes, products, procedures, or services that lead to some level of practical and valuable transformation. When you think of innovation, from here on out, it is important to remember that innovation comes in all shapes, sizes, flavors and colors. Remember there is not only one "type" or "kind" of innovation. And, remember one extremely important thing, innovation is more effective when it is radically people-centered.

In your review, it is important to remember the five sparks of a people-centered innovation atmosphere. These are five things you can immediately do to increase radical people-centered innovation within your organization. They are: 1) institutionalize creativity; 2) spotlight the maternity ward mentality; 3) play in the overlap; 4) allow for the meaningful collision of ideas; 5) ask innovation-sparking questions.

Also, in your review recall the 8 Brain Blocks that can put you, your employees, and your organization at a disadvantage when it comes to creative solution-discovery in the innovation process. 1) Incessant Drip; 2) Convenient Accessibility; 3) Option Obstruction; 4) Perceptual Presumptions; 5) Functional Fixedness; 6) Mental Set; 7) Confirmation Bias; and 8) Anchoring. But, recall, all is not lost, as you now know how to harness the immense power of your brain to stir new insight and uncover breakthroughs in your systems, technologies, processes, products, procedures, or services, as was addressed by using the mental power tool of submersive focus.

The final question to be asked and answered is: What now? The answer: start again. The information, tools, and questions found in this book can be used again and again. Just remember, that at the heart of innovation is the people within the organization. The employees within the organization are the very people who will spark the innovation, will implement the innovation, will iterate the innovation and who will sustain the innovation outcomes. The success of your organization may ultimately be in the hands of these employee-innovators, as they stimulate change and spark innovation within your organization. So, go ahead, provoke radical people-centered innovation in your organization.

About the Author

Corey Pruitt

 Speaker, author, and human performance strategist, Corey Pruitt is a thought leader in the areas of employee inspiration, employee engagement, employee innovation, leadership communication, learning and performance strategies. He is passionate about human performance in the workplace and sparking positive change in others.

Corey's unique blend of experiences in psychology (as a Family Therapist, Individual Counselor, Group Counselor, Crisis Counselor), business leadership (as a Director of Operations and Training, Training Analyst, Motivation/Performance Trainer, C-Suite, Entrepreneur), and higher education (Communication and Psychology Professor, Faculty Chair, Dean, Vice President & Chief Operating Officer) have set the foundation for his ability to motivate and transform individuals and organizations toward growth and lasting performance improvement.

Corey has obtained an undergraduate degree in Human Communication and a Master's degree in Psychology. He is finalizing his Doctorate in Leadership, with a research emphasis on a leader's influence on employee engagement and employee innovative behaviors. He also holds the following certifications:

- Certified in Advanced Motivational Interviewing and Behavior Change

- Certified Master Communicator

- Certified Performance Communicator

- Certified Neurolinguistic Practitioner

- Certified Prosci Change Management Practitioner

Corey has received numerous awards and recognition for his speaking, training and entertaining abilities. He is an established author of numerous books, articles, newsletters and blogs. As well, he is the founder and owner of multiple companies, including Iron Man Communications, Elite Illusions, Pruitt Consulting, LLC, the National Human Communication Institute, and most recently the founder and CEO of ChangeSparx, LLC.

Corey Pruitt

Other Spark-Related Products

Keynote Speaking and Training

Bring Corey to your organization to kick off your innovation initiative, or to lead your organization through the people-centered innovation process. Go to www.ChangeSparx.com to learn more.

Spark Tool Kit

Purchase the companion Spark Tool Kit, which includes a slide deck with the 52 ISQ's to use in your team meetings, a set of posters with the 52 ISQ's to promote them around your office, and a set of Spark journals with a place to write your individual brainstorms for each of the 52 ISQ's. Go to the marketplace at www.ChangeSparx.com to learn more.